CELEBRATIONS AND RITUALS

end-of-liferituals

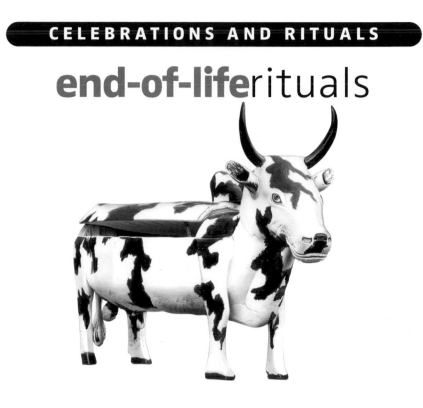

CHERRYTREE BOOKS

Published in the UK by Cherrytree Books, part of the
Evans Publishing Group
2A Portman Mansions
Chiltern Street
London W1U 6NR

First published in paperback in 2007.

In the same series:
Celebrating Prophets and Gods
Everyday Celebrations and Rituals
Marriage Celebrations
Winter Celebrations

British Library Cataloguing-in-Publication Data

Chambers, Catherine
End-of-life. – (Celebrations and rituals)
1. Funeral rites and ceremonies – Juvenile literature
I. Title II. Martell, Hazel Mary III. Morris, Neil
393

ISBN 978 1 84234 399 9

Printed and bound in China by C&C Offset
1 2 3 4 5 6 7 8 9 10 09 08 07 06 05 04 03

McRae Books:
Publishers: Anne McRae and Marco Nardi
Series Editor: Loredana Agosta
Graphic Design: Marco Nardi
Layout: Sebastiano Ranchetti
Picture Research: Claire Moore
Cutouts: Filippo delle Monache, Alman Graphic Design
Text: Catherine Chambers, Hazel Mary Martell, Neil Morris

Illustrations: Studio Stalio (Alessandro Cantucci, Fabiano
Fabbrucci, Andrea Morandi, Ivan Stalio), Ferruccio Cucchiarini, MM
Illustrazioni (Manuela Cappon) Paola Ravaglia, Paula Holguin,
Sabrina Marconi

Colour Separations: Litocolor, Florence (Italy)

Copyright © 2003, McRae Books Srl

Borgo La Croce, 8—Florence, Italy.
info@mcraebooks.com

Acknowledgements:
The Publishers would like to thank the following photographers
and picture libraries for the photos used in this book.
t=top; tl=top left; tc=top centre; tr=top right; c=centre;
cl=centre left; cr=centre right; b= bottom; bl=bottom left;
bc=bottom centre; br=bottom right
AFP: 15tr; A.S.A.P Picture Library: 28tr, 29cr; Corbis/Contrasto:
12br, 18tr, 19tr, 22b, 26cr, 27tl, 27br, 28bl, 32tr, 41br, 43br ; Lonely
Planet Images: Susan Storm 14cr, Susan Storm 14bl, Mason
Florence 18bl, Tony Wheeler 21tr, Neil Wilson 22c, Hannah Levy
25t, Hannah Levy 25cl, Bill Wasserman 31br, Stuart Wasserman
36bl, Patrick Syder 39cr, Peter Ptschelinew 43tl; Marco Lanza:
15bc, 37bl; The Image Works: 16br, 17tr, 17b, 20br, 23br, 31cl,
32bl, 33tr, 35cl, 35bl, 36cl, 37tr, 38br, 39br, 40tr

end-of-life rituals

CHERRYTREE BOOKS

Table of Contents

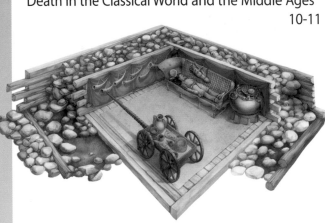

End-of-Life Rituals

Introduction

In most cultures and societies around the world, the death of a loved one not only causes great sadness but also typically involves special rituals. Burial has existed since prehistoric times. Sometimes people were buried with treasures and goods to help them in the afterlife. The deceased were often laid to rest in elaborate tombs and chambers. Burial is still a common way to dispose of the dead in the modern world, and in many traditional societies, it is the only way. Other ways of disposing of the dead are as diverse as cremation, sky burials and exposure in the Parsi Towers of Silence. Many societies follow traditional funeral rites and practices. In China, this may involve burning paper money or possessions for the deceased to use in the afterlife. In traditional Papua New Guinean societies, mourning wives smear their faces with mud. Funerals may consist of a short procession to the cemetery with the body wrapped in a simple white cloth or a great ceremony marking the death of a king or queen. In many parts of the world, the spirits of the dead are highly respected and honoured with festivals and feasts. These range from the cheerful O-Bon Festival in Japan, to the more serious Day of the Dead in Mexico.

Toy skeletons, *like the one at the far left, are popular with children in Mexico. On the Day of the Dead, Mexicans enjoy making fun of death. At the same time they never forget to honour their ancestors.*

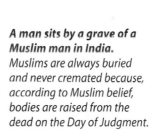

A man sits by a grave of a Muslim man in India. *Muslims are always buried and never cremated because, according to Muslim belief, bodies are raised from the dead on the Day of Judgment.*

An ancient Mesopotamian harp *was found in a queen's tomb, along with 23 servants who were buried with her. Ancient Mesopotamians strongly believed in an afterlife. They built lavish tombs for their kings and queens and filled them with precious possessions for use in the next world.*

END-OF-LIFE RITUALS
ANCIENT EGYPTIANS *bodies mummified*
CHINESE *Hungry Ghost Festival*
ETRUSCANS *duels at funeral ceremonies*
EUROPEANS *Halloween*
GA PEOPLE *fantasy coffins*
INCA *bodies dried out in mountain air*
INDIANS *funeral pyres*
IRISH *wakes to celebrate dead person's life*
JAPANESE *O-Bon Festival*
JEWS *stones laid on graves*
MAORIS *tangihanga ritual*
MEXICANS *Day of the Dead*
NEANDERTHALS *burial in shallow graves*
NORTH AMERICANS *shrines*
PARSI *funerals at Tower of Silence*
PLAINS INDIANS *scaffold burials*
TIBETANS *Sky Burials*
VIETNAMESE *mourners wear white*
VIKINGS *ship burials*

Death in Prehistoric and Ancient Cultures

The mummy of Rameses II, an ancient Egyptian ruler who died in 1213 B.C., lies in its coffin.

This wooden panel found in an Ur grave is decorated with a scene of men riding off to battle. It may have been part of a musical instrument.

Prehistoric people began making graves for their dead probably around 100,000 years ago, during the Old Stone Age, which ended about 35,000 years ago. At this time, people may have started believing in a life after death. Many ancient tombs contained weapons, jewellery, food, clothing and other objects. Scholars believe these grave-goods may have been intended to help the dead in the afterlife. Beginning around 2700 B.C., the ancient Sumerians and Egyptians developed more elaborate burial practices that included stone tombs.

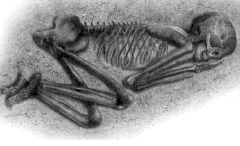

In early burials, the body was often laid on one side.

Ancient Rituals

Neanderthal Burials

The Neanderthals were early human beings who lived in parts of Europe, Southwest Asia and northern Africa between 130,000 and 35,000 years ago. Modern archaeologists have found evidence that Neanderthals buried their dead in shallow graves. Some were buried alone, others in groups. In some cases, stone tools, animal bones and even flowers have been found in or near Neanderthal graves.

The Royal Graves of Ur

The ancient city of Ur (in present-day Iraq) reached the height of its importance around 2500 B.C. The people of the region, called Sumerians, buried their dead kings and queens in royal graves. The graves also contained the remains of many servants, along with oxen, carts, gold and silver jewellery and precious stones. The servants probably were sacrificed so that they could continue tending their masters in the afterlife.

A head covering from a full jade suit used to bury a local king near Beijing.

Ancient China

Shi Huangdi, the first emperor of China, who died in 210 B.C., built a spectacular tomb for himself. It contained an army of nearly 8,000 life-sized soldiers and horses made of terra-cotta (baked clay). During the Han Dynasty (202 B.C. – A.D. 220), emperors and their families were buried in suits made of jade, a precious stone symbolising healing, good fortune and immortality.

Part of Emperor Shi Huangdi's "terra-cotta army."

Egyptian embalmers place a gilded mask over the head of a bandaged mummy prepared for burial.

Tombs and Pyramids of Ancient Egypt

The Egyptians firmly believed in the afterlife, and they devoted great energy and resources to preserving the bodies of the dead. Bodies were embalmed (preserved) then wrapped in linen bandages. The mummies were placed in wooden coffins. Rich people were also placed in tombs. Some dead pharaohs (Egyptian kings) were placed in burial chambers inside pyramids, such as the Great Pyramid at Giza. Rich people also had small wooden figurines placed in their tombs to act as servants in the afterlife.

EGYPTIAN EMBALMERS first removed the dead person's internal organs. The brain was pulled out through the nose, but the heart was left in the body. They stuffed the cavities with linen, then soaked the body with a chemical called natron to dry it out.

The Inca

The Inca, who lived high in the Andes Mountains along the western coast of South America, dried dead bodies in the thin, dry mountain air. Wealthy individuals were then wrapped in fine clothes and placed in a stone vault. Men were buried with hunting weapons, while women were buried with baskets. The dead were also entombed with gold and silver objects, as well as food and drink. The mummies of Inca emperors were kept in their former palace and sometimes put on display at festivals.

A small Inca statue found next to the body of a boy was probably intended to escort him to the next world.

This Inca man died more than 1,300 years ago. His body was mummified, then buried in a crouching position.

Celtic Beliefs

The Celts believed that when they died, their souls left their bodies and travelled to a magic world of spirits. They were buried with objects that would be useful on the journey and in the next world. Some important Celts were buried in wood-lined chambers under huge earthen mounds.

A wealthy Celt is laid out on a bronze couch, and his wagon is buried with him in the chamber.

This box from the 1100s was used as a reliquary, a container for the bones and objects belonging to a saint (holy person).

Death in the Classical World and the Middle Ages

Many of the funeral rituals of early Greece and Rome survived into later Western cultures. Both burial and cremation were practised in the classical world and were accompanied by processions and other mourning rituals. The tombs and coffins of wealthy people were elaborate, as shown by Etruscan examples. Hasty burials in common graves were more typical during periods of plague in the Middle Ages when millions died. By the time of the artistic rebirth of the Renaissance in the A.D. 1400s, tombs of the high-born and wealthy again became more and more magnificent.

This Etruscan coffin shows a married couple reclining on a couch.

Etruscan Fighters

The Etruscans, who flourished in central Italy from about 800 to 200 B.C., had a passion for sporting competitions. They developed a tradition of staging fights at funeral ceremonies. The blood they spilled served as a sacrifice to the spirit of the deceased. Later, such duels were held in memory of the dead.

THE ANCIENT ROMANS USUALLY HELD THEIR FUNERALS AT NIGHT. Funeral processions were often led by musicians, followed by women singers. Then came actors wearing masks of the dead person's family ancestors.

Early Christians painted the walls of the catacombs with scenes from the Bible.

Classical Greece

The Greeks either buried their dead or burned them on funeral pyres then buried the ashes. Burials took place outside cities, and graves often lined the roads beyond city walls. Rich people sometimes marked graves with a large decorated vase. On the third day of the annual festival of Anthesteria, people offered food to the spirits of the dead. The spirits supposedly returned to Earth each year on that day.

A scene from a Greek funeral vase shows a dead woman surrounded by mourners.

Christian Catacombs

Because Roman law did not allow burial within a city, early Christians buried their dead in niches in the walls of long underground chambers just outside Roman cities. Rome had more of these underground chambers, called catacombs, than any other city. Scholars estimate that six million Christians were buried in the catacombs around Rome. The word catacomb comes from the Greek words kata kumbas, which mean in the low place.

This is a reconstruction of a Viking ship that was used for burying a Viking queen in Norway around A.D. 850.

Viking Ship Burial

Rich Vikings often were buried with treasure for use in the afterlife. Some were even buried in a ship. The Vikings believed that the dead person could use the ship to sail to the next world. It also contained weapons, armour, tools and clothes as well as food and drink. Although the ships were usually buried under mounds, they were sometimes set on fire to make a funeral pyre. Other Viking burial sites were marked by stones arranged in the shape of a ship.

The tomb of Prince Edward, (1330–1376), heroic son of King Edward III of England and known as the Black Prince, is in Canterbury Cathedral. Many important people, such as kings, queens and members of their family, were buried in churches.

Places of Pilgrimage

The tombs of famous people, especially saints and religious leaders, often have become a destination for pilgrims from all over the world. Millions of Muslims visit Muhammad's tomb in Medina during their pilgrimage to Mecca, Islam's holiest city. According to Catholic tradition, St. Peter's Basilica, in Vatican City was built on the spot where St. Peter was buried. Many Christian tombs were designed and decorated by famous artists.

The Black Death

A terrible plague called the Black Death struck Europe, western Asia and northern Africa in the 1300s. Europe was the hardest hit, losing at least a third of its population. People contracted the disease after being bitten by fleas that had picked up the deadly plague bacteria from infected rats. At the time, however, most people thought the plague was caused by bad air or was a punishment from God. The terrible death toll created a preoccupation with death, and this was made worse by further outbreaks in later centuries. Because the plague was seen as a punishment from God for people's sins, many people performed rituals and ceremonies to repent for their sins and to ask God for his forgiveness and mercy. Groups of hooded Christians, called Flagellates, in white robes would walk in processions through the streets beating themselves with whips studded with iron spikes. They believed that this was a way to make up for the sins of humankind.

Ritual self-punishment causing bodily harm was called flagellation. It was practised throughout Europe by many Christians. It was later banned by Pope Clement VI in 1349.

The Black Death wiped out whole families and villages. So many people died that survivors had to bury the corpses in mass graves. Survivors often burned victims' belongings because they were contaminated.

Stone tablet— inscribing a person's name on a tablet ensures that the person's soul will reside there forever, according to Chinese tradition.

The Far East

Funeral Rituals in China

Care of the dead and of ancestors has always been an important part of Chinese folk religion. Since ancient times, the Chinese have worshipped and honoured their ancestors, making offerings at ancestral shrines. They believe it is their responsibility to look after the spirits of the dead and that this will bring them good fortune in their own lives. Over the centuries, ancestor worship became mingled with the teachings and rituals of Taoism, Confucianism and Buddhism. Today, many funerals contain elements from all these traditions.

A clay rooster found in a tomb from the time of the Eastern Han dynasty (A.D. 25–220) was intended to symbolically provide "food" for the deceased.

A decorated hearse is used to carry the coffin to the cemetery.

A coffin is lowered into a grave at a Chinese burial ceremony. Both mourners and grave workers are dressed in white robes. White is the colour of mourning in China.

Burial or Cremation?

Although Chinese Buddhists usually practise cremation, most Chinese prefer to bury their dead. They believe that a dead person's bones should be preserved. Burial promotes the decomposition (breaking down) of flesh while leaving behind the bones. Cemeteries are often found on hillsides, and most people believe that higher gravesites are more desirable than those lower down.

Cremation, practised since ancient times, is still the most common way of disposing of corpses among certain Buddhist ethnic minority groups. They follow this practice because Buddha himself was cremated.

THE FAR EAST

The Far East is the easternmost part of Asia. Asia extends from Africa and Europe in the west to the Pacific Ocean in the east. The northernmost part of the continent is in the Arctic. In the south, Asia ends in the tropics near the equator. Traditionally, the term Far East has referred to China, Japan, North Korea, South Korea, Taiwan and eastern Siberia in Russia. Southeast Asia includes Borneo, Brunei, Cambodia, East Timor, Indonesia, Laos, Malaysia, Myanmar, the Philippines, Singapore, Thailand and Vietnam.

Tablets or portraits of different ancestors are part of the ancestral shrines placed in the main hall of Chinese homes. Family members kneel and pray before them.

Mao Zedong (1893–1976) set up the People's Republic of China in 1949.

Spirit Offerings and Hell

Most Chinese believe that after death a person's soul descends to hell, where there are ten courts and ten judges. In each court, the soul is punished for its evil actions in life, before being allowed to pass on to the next court and, finally, heaven. The living can assist the souls by burning paper money as an offering to the judges. Goods placed in the coffin may also help the deceased on the journey and in the afterlife. These may include personal items, blankets and food.

Traditional Rites

Because white is the colour of mourning in China, white banners may be hung on a house to announce a death. People send flower wreaths of white or yellow (the colour of dignity) in memory of the deceased. Red flowers, symbolising happiness and good luck, are acceptable for those who lived a long life of at least 80 years. An inscribed stone or wooden tablet may be placed in the dead person's home to help his or her soul find its way back. If the deceased is buried, mourners turn away as the coffin is lowered into the ground to avoid bad luck. The traditional period of mourning is 100 days.

This Judge of the Dead is one of ten judges worshipped as gods by many Chinese people.

Communist Doctrine

The ruling Chinese Communist Party disapproves of traditional beliefs in spirits and the afterworld. It has tried to replace costly funeral services and burials with simple memorial meetings and cremation. According to party rules, black armbands for men and white cloth flowers for women should replace traditional mourning clothes of coarse cloth and drab colours. The new rules have been widely adopted in Chinese cities, but they have faced resistance in rural areas.

At this traditional funeral, relatives burn a paper chair for the deceased to use in the afterlife. Paper objects are often burned during funeral rites as an offering to the underworld judges and to ensure a safe passage to heaven for the deceased.

Fake money is often burned during the Hungry Ghost Festival to appease restless spirits.

Elaborate make-up, beautiful costumes and fancy headgear are all part of the street opera tradition. Performers, like this one from Singapore, try to please the hungry ghosts.

Hungry Ghost Festival

This festival is celebrated on the 15th day of the seventh month in the Chinese lunar calendar (around the end of August on the Western calendar). At this time, people look after the spirits that are not cared for by their families. These may be spirits of people who died without descendants or were not properly buried or who died in an accident. In several Southeast Asian countries, people feed and entertain the hungry ghosts, who are thought to roam during the seventh month, to make sure that they do no harm. Parents caution their children to return home before dark during the month.

Performances include a form of Chinese street theatre in which traditional characters act out popular folk tales, myths and legends.

This display was specially created as an offering to the hungry ghosts, who are presented with a variety of food and drink. The offering is intended to keep the spirits happy and occupied so that they will not cause mischief.

Offerings and Performances

Items burned as offerings to the ghosts include such paper gifts as pretend money and models of servants and cars. People also light candles and incense before bowing down to worship the spirits. Food is placed outside homes and in roadside displays. The hungry ghosts may be offered meat, rice, sweets or vegetables (see recipe on page 15). Performers attempt to please the ghosts with singing, dancing and theatrical performances. These productions are very serious affairs that often take place at dusk.

Water Lanterns

Water lanterns are a special tradition in Hong Kong and Taiwan. People make or buy the beautifully decorated paper lanterns, which are loaded onto model boats. On the evening before the start of the Hungry Ghost Festival, the lanterns are lit and put out to sea. They bring good luck and allow wandering or lost ghosts to find their way to land, so that they can enjoy the offerings made to them. After the lanterns have been released, priests bless the festival.

A large burning lantern is pushed out into a fishing harbour at Chi-lung, in Taiwan.

Bamboo grows tall and straight, producing thick stems. Bamboo-climbing contestants climb up bare poles that have been defoliated and erected in clusters on a platform.

The Legend of Mu Lian

A number of legends are connected with the festival. One of the most famous concerns a young man named Mu Lian who lived long ago. Mu Lian was a kind person, but his mother was wicked. She was mean to people and tortured animals. When the mother died, she was sent to hell, where she starved and suffered. Mu Lian was so upset that he asked Buddha for advice. Buddha told the young man to make offerings to the ghosts on the 15th day of the seventh month. When Mu Lian did this, his mother's suffering ended, and this was the beginning of the Hungry Ghost Festival.

Mu Lian is a character from Buddhist legend.

Bamboo Climbing

In Taiwan, a special competition is held on the last day of the seventh lunar month to scare away any ghosts that have not returned to hell. Contestants try to climb tall bamboo stems about 16 metres (52 feet) high attached to a special platform. To make the climb even more difficult, the bamboo is greased with beef fat. Offerings, such as meat and rice dumplings, are hung on the poles, and the climbers throw these down to the crowd. The first climber to collect a flag from the top of a pole is the winner.

10-VARIETY VEGETABLES

- 4-6 dried mushrooms
- 350 g tofu (bean curd)
- 60 g green beans
- 125 g each Chinese bok choy, cauliflower, courgettes, carrots, white mushrooms, fresh bean sprouts
- 60 g water chestnuts
- 3 ½ tablespoons vegetable oil
- 1 teaspoon salt
- 1 teaspoon sugar
- 2 tablespoons light soy sauce
- 1 teaspoon sesame oil

Soak the dried mushrooms for 30 minutes in warm water, then squeeze them dry (saving the water), discard the stalks and cut them in half. Cut the tofu into small pieces and put them in boiling water for 2 to 3 minutes. Drain well. Trim and wash the vegetables and cut into bite-sized pieces. Heat half of the vegetable oil in a pan and lightly brown the tofu. Heat the remaining vegetable oil and stir-fry the vegetables for 2 minutes. Add the tofu with the salt, sugar, soy sauce and some mushroom water. Stir, cover, reduce the heat and simmer for 4 to 5 minutes. Drizzle with sesame oil.

Japanese Funerals and the O-Bon Festival

In Japan, the ancient religion of Shinto mingles with Buddhist beliefs. Although many families follow Shinto tradition when celebrating birthdays, most people follow Buddhist funeral practice. Japanese people have great respect for their ancestors, whose spirits are thought to have power over the living. Family graves are well kept and always visited during one of the most important festivals of the year—the O-Bon, often called the Festival of the Dead or the Lantern Festival.

Many people in Japan still wear the traditional kimono on festival days and other special occasions.

People offer sympathy to a bereaved family by giving money in a condolence envelope, above right. *The special envelope, tied with black-and-white cords, is delivered to the funeral. The family later responds with a token gift.*

A priest leads a funeral procession to the cemetery, right. *A daughter of the deceased carries (right) a photograph of her father, and a son carries the urn of ashes in a box.*

THE WORLD OF THE DEAD

According to Shinto mythology, the god Izanagi, and his sister Izanami, created the world. They had many children who became the gods of nature. Izanami died after she gave birth to the fire god. The grief-stricken Izanagi then visited Yomi, the world of the dead, in an attempt to bring Izanami back. At the entrance of the dark place of Yomi he met Izanami. She told him that she could not leave because she had already eaten the food of Yomi, but she suggested that she discuss the matter with the gods of the underworld. Before going back she warned him not to follow and begged him not to look at her. Izanagi did not respect her wishes. He entered and lit a torch and discovered her decaying body covered with maggots. He fled with fright. Izanami became angry and sent evil hags and the eight gods of thunder, who guarded her body, after him. Izanagi managed to escape and sealed the entrance of Yomi with a huge boulder.

One of the eight gods of thunder. Since Izanagi was able to defend himself from the evil hags with magic, Izanami ordered the eight gods of thunder, along with the soldiers of Yomi, to capture him. They, too, failed.

A Japanese Funeral

Most Japanese funeral services follow Buddhist tradition. First, a Buddhist priest recites passages from the sutras (sacred Buddhist literature) while relatives burn incense sticks on the family altar. The dead person's body is then cremated. Afterward, close relatives may pick the bones out of the ashes, using chopsticks to pass them from person to person. The remains are placed in an urn and taken home to be put beside the family altar. 49 days after the death, the urn is taken to a cemetery to be placed with the remains of ancestors under the family stone.

Preparation for O-Bon

During the week before O-Bon, which is usually celebrated from the 13th to the 15th of either July or August, people give their house a good cleaning. Everyone travels home to be with their family and visit the family grave at least once. They hang paper lanterns painted with the family crest so that ancestral spirits can find their way to the grave site. At home, lanterns and fires are lit and doors are left open to welcome the spirits. Family members may enjoy a special meal, as this may be one of the few times in the year when they are all together. Then they are ready for O-Bon, which is always a joyous occasion.

Lanterns and candles are a major feature of the festival, which ends with a water display.

This Buddha statue has been decorated with vegetables and flowers for O-Bon. The cucumber on sticks represents a horse for the spirits to ride on.

O-Bon Celebrations

For three days, most people return to their birthplace, where they believe their ancestors' spirits will also return. The spirits are welcomed and honoured. They are offered rice cakes, vegetables and fruit. Some food is laid out on the family altar at home. One of the great highlights of the festival is the Bon-Odori (Dance for the Dead). People of all ages move slowly in a large circle around a wooden platform decorated with lanterns. The dance is full of solemn, graceful movements, so the dancers do not startle the spirits. On the last evening of the festival, people send their ancestors' spirits back to the other world in paper boats sailed on lakes and rivers. In many places, a fireworks display caps the celebration.

Girls performing the Bon-Odori usually wear a light cotton kimono as they dance to the music of drums and flutes.

Funeral Rituals in Vietnam and Thailand

A Buddhist temple in Thailand sometimes holds the bodies of important individuals for up to a year. Special religious rites are performed for the deceased at certain times of the year.

Buddhism is the major religion in these Southeast Asian countries. The vast majority of Thai people are Buddhists, while most Vietnamese follow a combination of Buddhism, Confucianism and Taoism. Although customs vary, funeral rites are considered extremely important and are usually elaborate. Families typically rely on Buddhist monks to chant for the deceased and conduct funeral services. These ceremonies are more festive than sorrowful. Grief is more openly displayed if the deceased was very young or died under tragic circumstances.

Vietnamese mourners in white ceremonial dress light candles on a coffin.

Funeral Clothing

In Vietnam, some of the deceased's clothes are folded neatly and placed inside the coffin. Mourners traditionally wear white clothes, which often differ according to the wearer's relationship to the deceased. The closest family members might wear white long-sleeved shirts and trousers and tie a piece of white fabric around their forehead. More distant relatives might simply wear a white scarf. The men who carry the coffin traditionally wear black. Elders of the community who are older than the deceased do not wear any special type of clothing.

A colourfully decorated hearse carries a coffin in a Vietnamese funeral procession.

Funeral Preparations in Vietnam

When a person dies, his or her body is wrapped in a white blanket and placed on a straw mat on that person's bed. The deceased's head rests on a pillow so that it can be seen by others and the person appears to be peacefully asleep. Money, gold or rice are usually placed in the dead person's mouth, so that he or she does not leave this life poor or hungry. Lit incense and a bowl of bananas, which Vietnamese Buddhists consider the most sacred fruit, are placed on a table next to the bed.

Thai Rituals

Relatives try to focus a dying person's mind on Buddhist scriptures. After the person has died, the relatives perform a washing ceremony by pouring scented water over the deceased's right hand. The body is then placed in a coffin decorated with flowers. Friends come to offer wreaths, incense and garlands. The body may be cremated within a day, though usually prayers and chanting continue for a week before the cremation. At a traditional funeral, friends and relatives place lit torches and candles beneath the coffin to light the funeral pyre. Incense is also burned.

Decorations for funeral pyres are made in the shape of traditional temples in Thailand.

Hmong women make burial clothes for themselves and their husbands. This set of male burial clothes is richly embroidered and includes a sash. Women wear special embroidered collars.

Among the Hill Tribes of Thailand

The people of the mountainous region of northern Thailand have their own special customs. Among the Hmong people, the dead are buried in special funeral clothes. After a chicken has been sacrificed, a village elder says a prayer for the dead person, who is believed to follow the chicken to the land of the Hmong ancestors. Then one man blows on reed pipes, while another beats a ceremonial death drum. During the funeral procession, a girl carries a burning torch to lead the way. Then she throws the torch down and runs home, so that the soul of the dead will be confused and not return to the village. For the Akha people, funerals tend to be lengthy occasions. For three nights and two days, a spirit priest, called a pi ma, performs death rites over the body. Then the coffin is carried on long poles to the burial ground. The Akha people think of death as a transition from the living world to that of the ancestors.

BAD DEATH
The Akha people consider certain causes of death, including being killed by a leopard, dying of smallpox or drowning, as bad. When this happens, a dog is killed and buried over the body to make sure the deceased doesn't start calling out from the grave.

A curved coffin holding the body of an elder is carried by people of the Akha tribe of northern Thailand to a burial site away from the village. The coffin was carved from a single log.

This Hindu goddess with many arms has different names to represent the passage of time and death. When she is called Kali, above, she represents destruction.

Hindu Funeral Rituals

There are about 750 million Hindus in the world, most of whom live in India and other countries of South Asia. Hindus have several gods, including Yama, the god of death, for whom they perform ceremonies, known as samskaras, throughout their lives. The final samskara, called Antyeshti, is performed for a person at death. It ensures that the soul begins its journey to the next world and does not remain trapped on Earth as a restless ghost after the body is cremated.

Sometimes patterns are painted on the soles of the dead person's feet.

South and Central Asia

Death Rituals

A Hindu who has died is positioned with his or her head pointing south, which is the direction Yama comes from. Sacred Hindu songs are sung and a few drops of water from the River Ganges are poured into the person's mouth. The body is bathed and dressed in new white clothes.

The eldest son or oldest male relative lights the funeral pyre on all four sides.

Death and Funeral Preparations

After being bathed and dressed, the body is tied onto a bamboo bier and placed in an open space. Women and children say prayers for the departed soul, then the dead person's oldest son covers the body with a cloth. The cloth, which is unbleached and uncut, is considered very pure. The son then leads the procession to the cremation area. Carrying a pot of water, he is followed by the bier and all the male relatives in descending order of age. In some processions, people blow horns, play cymbals and beat drums as they walk along.

A body is cremated by the River Baghmati at Kathmandu. The Baghmati is Napal's sacred river.

Funeral Pyre

At the cremation ground, a place is chosen and purified with water. After evil spirits are scared away by chanting, a pyre is built from logs. The body is prepared for the journey ahead by having its hair and nails trimmed and being bathed again. It is then laid on the pyre, once more with its head to the south. Purifying gold is placed on its lips, then more logs are piled on it. The oldest son walks three times around the pyre, sprinkling water from the pot he has brought, before dropping and breaking it by the dead person's head. He then lights the pyre while a priest prays to Agni, the god of fire.

SOUTH AND CENTRAL ASIA

South and Central Asia are areas of distinct cultures and peoples. These regions form an area at the base of Asia. Asia extends from Africa and Europe in the west to the Pacific Ocean in the east. The northernmost part of the continent is in the Arctic. In the south, Asia ends in the tropics near the equator. South Asia is made up of Afghanistan, Armenia, Bangladesh, Bhutan, India, the Maldives, Nepal, Pakistan, Sri Lanka, the Tibetan plateau in southwest China and parts of the countries of Azerbaijan and Georgia. Much of India, the largest country in south Asia, forms a peninsula that extends southward into the Indian Ocean. Central Asia includes the countries of Kazakhstan, Kyrgyzstan, Tajikistan, Turkmenistan, Uzbekistan and the West Siberian Plain.

Varanasi Pilgrimage

Varanasi (formerly Benares) is the most sacred Indian city on the banks of the River Ganges. Traditionally called Mahashamshana (the great cremation ground), it is the favourite place for Hindus to be cremated. They believe cremation at that special place will liberate them from the endless cycle of birth, death and rebirth. Many go to Varanasi with the intention of dying there and are known as Jivan Muktis, meaning those who are liberated while still alive.

Pollution and Purification

Once the funeral pyre is lit, the mourners bathe in the river, then throw handfuls of water onto the fire as a last offering to the body. Two or three mourners stay until the body has burned to ashes, while the youngest male leads the others back to the dead person's home. Before going in, they purify themselves by touching such things as a stone, fire, oil or water. Family members enter what is considered a period of pollution, which lasts for 12 days after the death. During this period, offerings of food such as pindas are made to the dead person's soul as nourishment while the soul forms a new body. Also during these 12 days, the family must observe a number of restrictions, including a ban on cooking. They must rely on neighbours for their meals. Three days after the cremation, a relative of the dead person collects the bones and ashes.

Rice balls called pindas are placed near the body to provide nourishment for the dead person's soul.

Cremation fires burn day and night on the ghats (steps) along the banks of the River Ganges in Varanasi, India.

Sending the Soul

After the 12 days of pollution and purification, the body is provided with more food for the journey to the next world. Hindus who live in urban areas and cannot have traditional funerals have their cremations at the local crematorium. But the ashes are still collected and scattered on the River Ganges if possible.

The bowls of fire held by this woman are part of a purification process that mourners go through immediately after the funeral of a friend or relative. Purification takes place during a period of pollution in which the family comes to terms with their loss.

SUTTEE

Hindu widows in India used to practise an ancient custom known as suttee, in which she would throw herself into her husband's funeral pyre. It was believed that in this way she could follow him to the next life and be his companion. Although the practice of suttee was voluntary, many women felt pressured to do it and tried to escape. Women who practised suttee were highly respected. In some instances when a man's death was expected or imminent, his wife was often sacrificed before he died. It is believed that suttee became a widespread practice mainly because a widow in traditional society often faced many difficult life conditions, such as poverty, after her husband's death. Suttee was abolished in 1829 by Lord William Bentinck, the British ruler of India who, unlike other British rulers, did not hesitate to put a stop to this practice that was so deeply rooted in tradition and religious belief.

This illustration from a medieval Indian manuscript shows the wife of an Indian nobleman jumping into her husband's funeral pyre.

Parsi Rituals and Traditions

Two guards are shown watching over a fire altar. *Fire is sacred to the Parsis because it gives light, warmth and energy and helps create life.*

Parsis follow an ancient faith known as Zoroastrianism after its founder, Zoroaster or Zarathustra, who lived in what is now northeastern Iran. Many Parsis migrated to India between the A.D. 700s and 900s, settling mainly around Mumbai (formerly Bombay). They believe in one Supreme God, Ahura Mazda, creator and judge of the world. They believe a constant struggle exists between the twins Spenta Mainyu, the spirit of good, and Angra Mainyu, the source of darkness, death and evil. Zoroastrian worship is focused on the fire altar.

Parsis worship in fire temples, where the sacred fire burns day and night. Only priests are allowed into the inner chamber of the temple, where the fire altar is located.

Sandalwood and frankincense burn *for three days on the spot in the house where the body rested.*

SAGDID IS A PARSI RITUAL in which a dog is brought to watch over the corpse. Parsis believe that dogs can guide a person's soul from the body and into the world of the dead. They also believe that dogs can drive away demons that may be hovering around the dead person.

Parsi Death Rituals

When a Parsi is dying, two priests come to pray for the person to repent his or her sins. As payment, the priests receive corn and money from the family. The part of the house where the body will lie is washed with water. Because the cow is sacred in the Parsi religion, a corpse is first sprinkled with cow's urine. It is then washed with water, placed on a white sheet and covered with a clean white cloth. A sacred thread is placed round the corpse, and the relatives pay their last respects to the deceased.

The Tower of Silence

A traditional funeral takes place at a Tower of Silence, below, a huge, round stone structure with an opening on the top that sits on a hill or a high place outside a town. All who attend are dressed in white and walk silently in pairs behind two priests. When the last respects have been paid, the body is laid in a pit inside the tower and left partly uncovered to attract flesh-eating birds, such as black vultures.

Funeral Procession

After prayers have been said to give courage to the dead person's family, the relatives take a last look at the body. The corpse-bearers, called Nasasalars, then secure the body on the iron bier and take it out of the house to a second group of Nasasalars who will carry the body to the Tower of Silence.

THE JUICE OF A HAOMA PLANT is often poured into the mouth of a dying person. Haoma is considered a sacred plant by Parsis, a symbol of the soul's immortality.

Jainism in India

The Jain religion was founded in India in the 500s B.C., and approximately three million of its followers live there today. Jains believe that everyone goes through a continuing cycle of birth, death and rebirth. They believe people can be liberated from this cycle only by living a nonviolent life in which compassion, forgiveness, gratitude, truth and simplicity play an essential role. They are strict vegetarians and believe that it is important not to hurt any living thing, because even the tiniest creature has a soul.

This empty shape represents a siddha (liberated soul), which has escaped the cycle of death and rebirth.

Jains worship Tirthankaras, beings who have achieved enlightenment. Such icons are particularly worshipped during sacred rituals. This illustration shows Mahavira, the 24th Tirthankara.

Reincarnation Beliefs

Jains believe that although the body dies, the jiva (soul) lives on and is born again in another body. The new life might be better or worse than the previous one. To escape this cycle, they try to detach themselves from material possessions and use their wealth to build schools, hospitals and temples. They also treat all life with respect. Monks and nuns even wear masks to avoid killing tiny insects they might breathe in.

Jain Funerals

Ideally, a Jain hopes to die while fasting or meditating. The soul is thought to leave the body instantly upon death, and so cremation takes place as soon as possible. Mourners meditate during the cremation process. Then they collect the ashes and throw them into a river.

JAIN TEMPLE IN RAJASTHAN

Jain temples, such as this one in the state of Indian Rajasthan, are beautiful works of architecture, with rich carvings and decorations. They are dedicated to the 24 Tirthankaras or Jinas who were the founders of Jainism and whose teachings show their followers how to escape the cycle of reincarnation. Images of the Tirthankaras are found inside all Jain temples. Worshippers offer them food, drink, flowers, sandalwood and incense to honour their past life.

This ceremonial skull container reminds the living of Buddha's teaching that nothing lasts forever.

Tibetan Rituals and the Sky Burial

A Tibetan lama's (priest or monk) ritual headdress is worn at festivals and ceremonies. A lama performs a ritual to help a dead person's mind leave the body through the top of the head.

After Buddhism spread into Tibet around A.D. 650, Tibetans developed their own version of this religion, incorporating elements from an ancient religion called Bon. From 1578, a priest known as the Dalai Lama served as their religious and political leader. In 1959, the last Dalai Lama was exiled after trying to regain his country's independence from China. China, which took control of Tibet in 1951, banned many Tibetan traditions. Since the 1980s, however, the Chinese have been slightly more tolerant of Tibetan culture.

THE ROOF OF THE WORLD—Tibet is separated from the rest of the world by high mountains, and so it is known as The Roof of the World.

Buddha's funeral pyre. Because wood is scarce in Tibet, there are no coffins and only important lamas are cremated.

Dying

Traditionally, when a Tibetan is close to death, a lama comes to prepare him or her spiritually by chanting and surrounding the person with Buddhist images. Once death occurs, a white cloth is thrown over the person's face and no one is allowed to touch the body. Tibetans believe it takes three or four days for the soul to leave the body and complete the death process. During this time, the lama sits by the body, explains what will happen on the way to the afterlife, and tries to guide the deceased on the path toward its rebirth.

A damaru is a two-sided drum played along with a trumpet in a Tibetan funeral procession. Each side of the damaru represents a human skull, symbolising the dual nature of life— the spiritual and the physical.

Funerary Ritual

Before the funeral, friends and relatives gather at the dead person's house. They make offerings of food and drink to the dead person's spirit. On the third evening, they gather around the body and explain that, although it is no longer part of the household, it is still loved. Gifts and money are presented, and prayer scarves called hadas are placed on the body. Early the next morning, the lama leads the funeral procession to the burial ground. Family and friends follow for a short distance, carrying lighted incense sticks. Only a few of the closest relatives go all the way to the burial ground.

Prayer flags flutter over a Sky Burial ground. A Buddhist prayer appears on each of the flags. Often made of cotton, the flags are dyed blue, white, red, green or yellow—the colours representing the five Buddha families. Tibetans place the flags on the mountains to control the spirits that live there.

Lamps fuelled with yak butter burn for a dead person. These lamps are burned on the fourth and seventh weeks of mourning, either in a home or a monastery.

Sky Burial

Sky Burial is the name given to a traditional Tibetan way of disposing of a dead body. In fact, it is not a form of burial. Instead, the body is taken to a sacred site in the mountains where burial specialists called rogyapas cut it into pieces. They then strip the flesh from the bones and break up the bones with a hammer until the pieces are small enough to be eaten by the flocks of vultures that live in the area. The Chinese banned sky burial in the 1960s and 1970s but have allowed it again in a limited way since the 1980s.

IN BHUTAN IN THE HIMALAYAN MOUNTAINS, a person known as the Lord of Death performs a special dance to remind people that death dances among them, and they will all die one day. Bhutan lies directly south of Tibet.

Rituals After Death

Once a week for the first seven weeks after a death, Buddhist monks chant sutras to redeem the sins of the dead person. On the 49th day, family and friends gather again to offer hadas and money. During this mourning period, the family does not attend marriages or celebrate festivals.

There are five Buddhist monasteries on the 51-kilometre (32-mile) path around Mount Kailas.

MOUNT KAILAS

Mount Kailas in western Tibet is over 6,700 metres (22,000 feet) high. It is a spiritual centre for followers of four different religions—Tibetan Buddhism, Hinduism, Jainism and Bon, which is Tibet's traditional religion. Pilgrims have visited the mountain for centuries to achieve enlightenment and purification. People walk around it on a circular path that is 4,600 to 5,600 metres (15,000 to 18,000 feet) high. Breathing is difficult at this altitude, and some people take two to three weeks to complete the circuit. Others hire someone to do the pilgrimage for them, while the fittest use a special breathing technique to get around the mountain in just one day. Pilgrims often leave a piece of clothing, lock of hair or even a drop of blood there. In this way, they leave behind a part of themselves that they wish to give up.

Muslims believe that every person has two angels watching over him or her. The angels note the person's good and bad deeds, keeping a record for the Day of Judgment.

Muslim Rituals

Islam began in the Middle East after the Prophet Muhammad received revelations from God in the early A.D. 600s. It remains dominant in the region but has also spread throughout the world. Muslims—the followers of Islam—see death as part of their submission to the will of the one true God, Allah. They believe that when people die, they face the Day of Judgment. Believers who have led a good life are rewarded forever in paradise. According to the *Qur'an*, the holy book of Islam, paradise is a beautiful garden full of flowers and flowing water. Those who sin, however, must go to hell.

A beautifully inscribed page from an old **Qur'an.** *Many Islamic prayers for the dying and dead are taken from this holy book.*

Death

Muslims hope to die surrounded by their family and close friends. Relatives try to help a dying person by offering comfort, saying prayers and thinking of Allah. It is always best if the person last words are "La ilaha illa Allah", meaning "There is no God but Allah". When a person dies, the eyes are gently closed and a prayer is said. The body is ritually washed, if possible by a close relative of the same sex as the deceased. It is then wrapped in a shroud of white sheets.

A Muslim body is wrapped simply. Men are usually wrapped in three sheets, just as Muhammad was. Women, however, are generally wrapped in five or seven sheets.

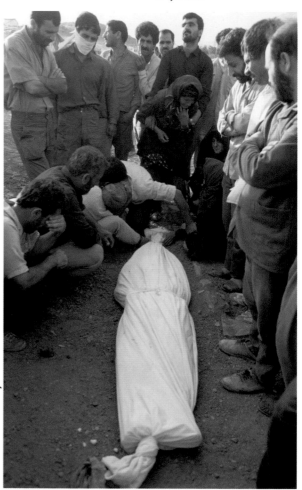

The Middle East

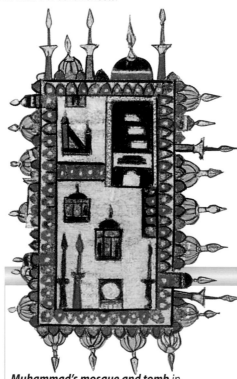

Muhammad's mosque and tomb in Medina are shown in this Moroccan illustration from the 1500s.

THE MIDDLE EAST

The Middle East covers parts of northern Africa, southwestern Asia and southeastern Europe. Scholars disagree on which countries make up the Middle East. But many say the region consists of Bahrain, Cyprus, Egypt, Iran, Iraq, Israel, Jordan, Kuwait, Lebanon, Oman, Qatar, Saudi Arabia, Sudan, Syria, Turkey, United Arab Emirates and Yemen. The region also is the birthplace of three major religions—Judaism, Christianity and Islam.

PILGRIMAGE TO MEDINA

The Prophet Muhammad died at his home in Medina in what is now Saudi Arabia, in A.D. 632. He died in his wife Aishah's arms and was buried at that very place. This site is now a shrine and has become a place of pilgrimage. Many Muslims visit the Prophet's tomb after their pilgrimage to Mecca, also in Saudi Arabia. Muslims are required to make this pilgrimage once in their lifetime if possible. Muslims are encouraged to make pilgrimages to other holy places, too.

A wrapped body is carried in a simple wooden coffin in a Muslim funeral procession.

This ceramic decoration is from the tomb of Ansari al-Harowi, a Muslim poet and saint who died in A.D. 1089. Important Muslims are often buried in tombs.

Burial

Muslim tradition forbids cremation, specifying that the body should be buried within a day after death. The wrapped body is usually carried to the cemetery. Mourners take turns carrying the body on their shoulders, four mourners at a time. People in the funeral procession do not wail or display grief loudly but show dignity and respect for the deceased. Although women are allowed at a Muslim funeral, their attendance is not encouraged. Traditionally, coffins are not used, but today some Muslims use a simple wooden coffin. If a coffin is used, the body is removed just before burial. The body is put in the grave on its right side, with the face toward Mecca. Wood or bricks are placed on top of the body so that the earth does not touch the body when the grave is filled in. Muslims believe the body should rest on the earth, instead of the earth resting on the body.

The Day of Judgment

Muslims believe that after a person dies there will be a Day of Judgment, when God will raise the dead person and judge that person's life. Believers who have led good lives will be rewarded in paradise, while all others will be sent to the fire of hell. Angels are believed to be God's messengers and they have important roles in the afterlife. The angel Israfil will

blow his horn to announce the Day of Judgment. Ridwan is the guardian of paradise, and Malik is the guardian of hell.

The angel Israfil blows his trumpet on the Day of Judgment.

Honouring the Dead

Islamic funerals and cemeteries are simple, never costly or showy. When a grave has been filled in, the surface of the earth is raised a little. Graves are usually marked with a simple headstone. A spouse mourns a husband or wife for four months and ten days. Otherwise, the period of mourning is three days and nights. Commemoration services are sometimes held 40 days after death or on the first anniversary of someone's death.

Muslims mourn the death of a family member at a cemetery in Iran. Muslim graves are usually very simple.

A special water jug is used for ritually washing a dead body.

Jewish End-of-Life Rituals

Jews believe that they have a special relationship with their one true God. Jewish traditions and rituals are very old, going back about 4,000 years to the time of the patriarch Abraham. Judaism was born in the Middle East. Today, traditional Jewish rituals are still followed in Israel, which was established as a Jewish homeland in 1948, as well as by Jews in other parts of the world. Jewish end-of-life rituals are simple but meaningful.

Jewish mourners carry a shrouded body to a cemetery in a detail from an old painting.

Before Burial

Soon after death, members of the herva kaddisha (burial society) wash the body, dress it in simple white clothing and wrap it in a white shroud. A man is usually dressed in his tallit (fringed prayer shawl). The shrouded body is put in a plain wooden coffin, and then watched over so that it is never left alone. Mourners take turns watching over the body, reciting psalms as they do so.

Men place a wrapped body in a wooden coffin at a burial in Galilee.

The Funeral and Mourning

According to Jewish law, burial should take place within 24 hours of death. Jewish law also forbids cremation or embalming because these acts are considered disrespectful. On the way to the cemetery, the funeral procession stops seven times to recite Biblical passages. Seven represents the seven days of creation described in Genesis in the Bible. Close relatives of the deceased make a small tear in their clothes as a sign of their grief. After the coffin has been lowered into the grave, family and friends take turns covering it with shovelfuls of earth before the grave is filled in. The family remains in mourning, called shiva, for seven days after the funeral. They stay at home and are visited by friends, who pray with them. On each yahrzeit (anniversary) of the death, a candle is lit in memory of the deceased.

Jewish men pray at a graveside. Funeral prayers in praise of God are recited in memory of the dead person.

YOM HASHOAH

After World War II (1939-1945), Israel established Yom HaShoah, a day to commemorate the victims of the Holocaust, the systematic murder of Jews and members of other minority groups by Nazi Germany. The word Holocaust means sacrificial offering by fire. At the command of German dictator Adolf Hitler, millions of Jews were sent to concentration camps, where many were killed in gas chambers. Their bodies were cremated or thrown into mass graves. By the end of the war, the Nazis had murdered six million people. Today Yom HaShoah is celebrated in April or May, around the time of the Warsaw Ghetto Uprising in 1943, in which Jewish fighters in Poland tried to resist the Nazis. Yom HaShoah is observed with poems, prayers, singing and candlelight. Often, six candles are lit to represent the six million victims of the Holocaust.

A monument commemorates the Warsaw Ghetto Uprising of 1943.

The Kaddish Prayer

Sons of the deceased recite the Kaddish, a hymn of praise to God, for 11 months and one day after the death of a parent. The prayer is often a plea for the coming of the Messiah, the anointed one chosen by God. Jews believe that with the coming of the Messiah, the dead will be resurrected and mankind will be judged.

A group of people lays stones on a relative's grave in a Jewish cemetery.

A large Jewish cemetery on the Mount of Olives overlooks the city of Jerusalem. It has existed since ancient times.

Stone Laying

In Biblical times, Jewish graves had tombstones without names, dates or any other engraving. A mound of earth was marked simply with a few rocks. As time passed, the rocks wore down. As a result, it became traditional for each visitor to the grave to add a single stone to the original pile so that the grave would always have a marker. This became a way for the living to remember and honour the dead.

Mary, the mother of Jesus, her sister Elizabeth, Mary Magdalene and the apostle James mourn over the body of Christ in an image from the 1400s.

The rosary is a string of beads used as an aid to memory and concentration while praying. A certain prayer is said while touching each bead. Early forms of praying using a rosary began in Christianity in the Middle Ages, becoming widespread in the 1400s and 1500s.

European Religious Traditions

A priest anoints a dying man with holy oil in a painting from the Middle Ages.

Christians believe that death does not signal the end of life. They believe that those who follow the teachings of Jesus will, as He promised, win eternal life in heaven. In most European countries, a funeral service commemorates the dead person, allows the family time to grieve and gives the deceased a religious blessing. Funeral services vary from country to country and can be as majestic as that of a king or queen or as simple as a quiet farewell attended by friends and family. Burial is still traditional in most Catholic countries, though cremation is becoming more common in Europe.

An Irish Wake

A traditional Irish wake, held both to celebrate a person's life and prepare the deceased for the next life, was common in much of Ireland until the 1970s. The ritual usually lasted from the time of death until the start of the funeral service. After the body was bathed and dressed in a white robe, it was laid on a bed or table. Rosary beads were placed in the dead person's hands. Visitors arrived to pay their respects to the deceased. In the past, keening (wailing) was a common feature of a wake and was thought to be a way of communicating with the dead person. A wake was also a time to share food and drink, play music and dance.

Last Rites

The Roman Catholic and Eastern Orthodox tradition of anointing the sick, called unction, has been practised for many centuries and is one of the seven sacraments of these churches. In the Middle Ages, people feared that if they did not confess their sins before dying, they might lose their place in heaven. Special services were held to help the dying or sick, and from these the ceremony of last rites developed. In this ritual, a priest offers the dying person an opportunity to make a final confession, and often anoints the person with holy oil, an ancient symbol of healing. Prayers are also said to prepare the dying person to meet with God.

Europe and the Americas

EUROPE

Europe is one of the smallest of the world's seven continents in area but one of the largest in population. Europe extends from the Arctic Ocean in the north to the Mediterranean Sea in the south and from the Atlantic Ocean in the west to the Ural Mountains in the east. The 47 countries of Europe include the world's largest country, Russia, as well as the world's smallest, Vatican City. Russia lies partly in Europe and partly in Asia.

Death Announcements

In many parts of southern Europe, posters are pasted on walls and buildings to announce a person's death. The black-and-white notices usually include the names of the dead person's family, funeral details and a short prayer or religious symbol.

Munita dei conforti religiosi ha reso l'anima a Dio

FRANCESCA PEPI

Ne danno il triste annuncio: il marito Luciano, i figli Lucio, Marco, Maria, Giuseppe e Rosa, i generi, le nuore, i fratelli, le sorelle, i cognati, le cognate, i nipoti ed i parenti tutti.

Le Esequie avranno luogo domani 22 ottobre alle ore 16:00 muovendo dalla casa dell'Estinta in via M. Malibran, 130 per la chiesa di S. Luca.

20 ottobre 2002

Royal Funeral

The death of a king or queen usually results in an elaborate funeral and a lavish display of pageantry and procession. When Queen Victoria of Great Britain died in 1901, British adults wore black clothes for three months, and black-and-purple banners were hung from windows. After a royal death, flags are flown at half-mast, condolence books are opened for people to write messages of memorial and the body often lies in state. During this time, the casket, draped in the king's or queen's flag with his or her crown on top, rests in a public place for a few days before the funeral service. Lying-in-state is typically reserved for rulers, heads of state and important citizens. In the funeral procession, soldiers in ceremonial uniform and members of the royal family (usually only males) join in a walking cortege behind the casket, as military bands play sombre music.

The crown of Queen Elizabeth was made for her when she and her husband, George VI, were crowned in 1937. It contains the famous Koh-i-noor diamond. It lay on top of her casket during the lying-in-state and her funeral service in April 2002.

Soldiers guard the coffin of Queen Elizabeth, the Queen Mother, as her body lies-in-state in Westminster Hall, London, before her funeral. Members of the public file past the casket to pay their respects.

THE GREEK TRADITION OF PUTTING A COIN IN THE POCKET OR MOUTH of a dead person dates back to ancient times. The coin was believed to pay for the dead person's journey to heaven.

A widow in southern Italy wears traditional black mourning clothes.

Martorana were originally made by the sisters of a Benedictine religious order in Palermo, on the island of Sicily, Italy. They are a traditional Sicilian sweet made to celebrate All Souls' Day.

Mourning Clothes

Black clothes are a common feature of most funeral services and mourning periods throughout Europe. However, in Italy, Greece, Spain, and other parts of southern Europe, many widows, usually older women, wear black clothes for the rest of their life as a sign of bereavement. Each of these women carefully tends her husband's grave, often making daily visits to the cemetery.

Festival of the Dead

All Souls' Day is celebrated on November 2 in many Roman Catholic countries. In honour of departed relatives, people attend mass, visit cemeteries and decorate graves. In Sicily, children believe that their dead relatives will return the night before All Souls' Day and leave them sweets and small toys. Martorana (marzipan candy in the shape of fruits) is prepared for this special day. In Spain, it is traditional to bake a loaf of bread for the occasion.

Commemorating Death in Europe

Europeans commemorate death in many ways that reflect differences in their ethnic and religious traditions. In Italy, funerals may require the use of an aquatic hearse, or may simply consist of a silent walking procession. Elegant tomb sculptures may be erected in memory of a loved one, and children enjoy the celebrations marking the ancient festival of the dead on Halloween. In many parts of Europe, people wear or display red poppies each November 11 in remembrance of the millions of soldiers killed in warfare over the years. Many European traditions and practices were taken by emigrants to other parts of the world.

After World War I, war memorials were built in most towns and villages in Europe. They remembered all those who had died in what was known as the Great War.

The poppy has become the symbol of all those who have died in war. Despite battles that devastated the landscape, poppies continued to grow in the fields of northern France and Flanders during World War I.

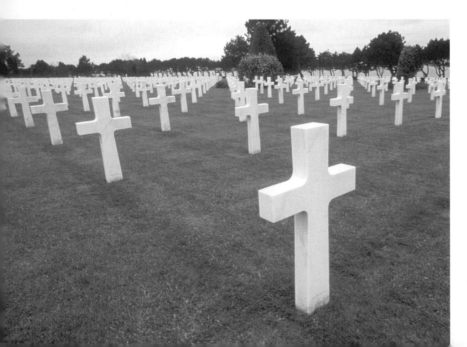

A Venetian funeral barge carries mourners across a canal.

Italian Funeral Processions

Funeral processions in Italy are solemn affairs, often involving much of the community, especially in smaller villages and towns. In many parts of southern Italy, a brass band plays an integral role in the procession, leading the casket and mourners through the streets to the church. In some parts of Sicily, people line the route of the funeral procession, slowly clapping as the casket passes to show their respect for the dead. In Venice, the city's cemetery sits on the island of San Michele. Elaborately decorated funeral gondolas carry caskets and mourners to the island.

Remembrance Day

November 11 was originally known as Armistice Day and commemorated all those who died in World War I (1914–1918). Its name was later changed to remember veterans of World War I and also all later conflicts. In many parts of Europe, wreaths of poppies, the international symbol of remembrance, are laid at war memorials, such as the Cenotaph in central London. A two-minute silence is also observed at 11 a.m. to mark the signing of the Armistice (the peace agreement between Germany and the Allies) on the 11th hour of the 11th day of the 11th month in 1918.

A famous military cemetery for the soldiers who died in World War II (1939-1945) lies in Normandy, northern France.

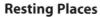

A sorrowful sculpture adorns a tomb in Père Lachaise Cemetery in Paris, France.

Resting Places

During the Middle Ages, Christians in Europe buried their dead beneath the floors or in the crypts (special rooms underground) of churches and cathedrals. But as this became increasingly impractical, they began building cemeteries in open areas near churches. Many of these cemeteries, such as the Père Lachaise Cemetery in Paris, are set on beautiful grounds and contain magnificent tombstones. There, graves belonging to the rich and famous, such as English writer Oscar Wilde and American rock star Jim Morrison, are visited by more than a million visitors each year, who also come to see the statues of grieving female figures that adorn many of the tombs.

Halloween

One of the oldest holidays, Halloween was originally known as Samhain and celebrated the eve of the ancient Celtic New Year. In early Christian times, it became All Hallow's Eve, a time to pray for dead saints. Old pagan beliefs saw Halloween as the only night of the year when spirits, witches and ghosts could wander freely. Today, Halloween is still celebrated on October 31 in much of Europe and North America, and children dress as ghosts, goblins, witches and other characters. They visit people's houses, saying "trick-or-treat" and collecting goodies. At Halloween, people create jack-o'-lanterns by hollowing out large pumpkins, cutting scary faces through the shell and putting a lighted candle inside.

Children dressed in Halloween costumes set out to collect sweets by trick-or-treating.

MAKE A GHOST COSTUME OR WITCH'S HAT

To make a ghost costume, first get permission to use a large white sheet. With an adult helping you, cut holes for your eyes in the sheet with scissors. Put the sheet over your head. Now you are ready to scare your friends on Halloween!

To make a witch's hat, take a piece of black card, twist it into a cone shape (see Fig. 1), and tape it. Use the other sheet of paper to draw around a large plate , then cut out the circle. Place the black cone onto the circle of paper and draw around it (see Fig. 2). Now cut a hole in the middle of the circle about 2 cm (1 inch) from the pencilled circle. Cut four small square pieces out of the inner circle (see Fig. 3). Place the base of the cone on top of the circle and glue the flaps of the circle to the outside of the cone (see Fig. 4).

Use a sheet of silver foil to cut out moon and star shapes to decorate your hat (see Fig.5). Enjoy!

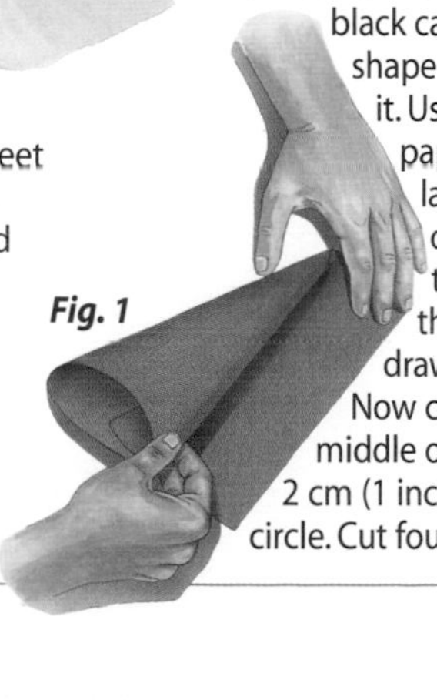

- a large, white bed sheet (get permission first)
- 2 sheets of black card
- scissors
- tape
- glue
- coloured pens
- a roll of silver foil
- a large plate

Fig. 1

Fig. 2

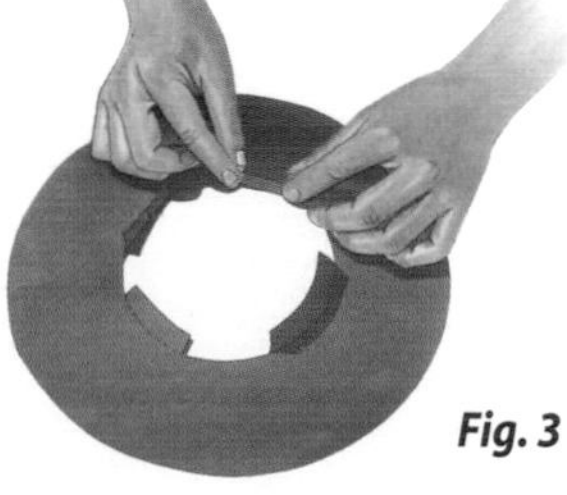

Fig. 3

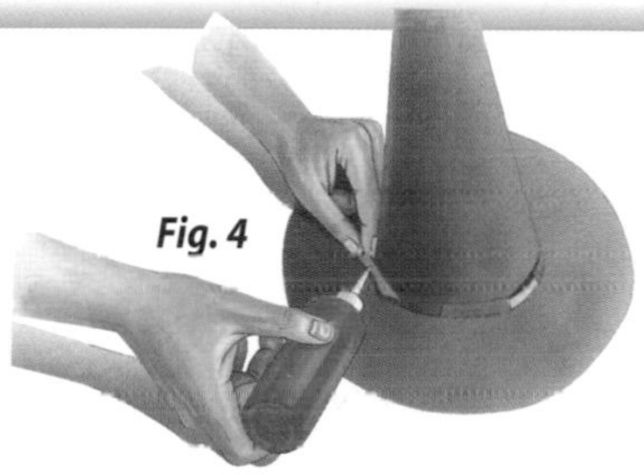

Fig. 4

Fig. 5

Decorated baskets are sometimes buried in American Indian graves or burned at mourning ceremonies. The basket above is covered with feathers and decorated with beads and shells.

A carved totem pole stands as a memorial to a dead Haida Indian of the Pacific Northwest. Some totem poles hold the remains or ashes of a person.

IN ARLINGTON NATIONAL CEMETERY, in Virginia, the Tomb of the Unknown Soldier has military guards all year round. At this spot, three unknown soldiers are buried: two from each World War and one from the Korean War.

End-of-Life Rituals for North Americans

Funeral rituals and burial customs have varied throughout American Indian culture, according to their view of death and the afterlife as well as the environment. Some tribes built large burial mounds and ceremonial centres. On the plains and in the mountains, bodies were often buried in caves or put up on scaffolds or in trees. In the Pacific Northwest, wooden posts sometimes held the remains of the dead. In desert areas, the deceased were often cremated. In modern North American culture, rituals surrounding death often reflect immigrant ethnic and religious traditions. Some graves have become popular tourist sites. Providing funeral services has become "big business".

American Indian Burial

The Plains people strongly believed in an afterlife. Some buried their dead in the earth, but most preferred to place dead bodies high above the ground, where they would be safe from animals. They put up a scaffold made of four posts and placed the wrapped body at the top. When the scaffolds decayed, the bones were buried in rock crevices or caves. Some Pueblo peoples rubbed the body of the deceased with a powder made from corn before burial. This ritual marked the individual's transition from the world of the living to the world of the supernatural.

Huron Feast of the Dead

The Feast of the Dead was an important festival among the Huron people of the eastern woodlands. It was held once every ten years, when the remains of all those who had died during the previous decade were collected. During the ten day festival, any remaining flesh and clothes on the body were burned. The bones were placed in beaver-skin bags. They were then re-buried in a mass grave, together with such objects as pipes, pots and beads. At the end of the festival, the grave was covered and wooden posts were placed around it.

THE AMERICAS

The continents of North America and South America make up the Western Hemisphere. North America contains Canada, Greenland, the United States, Mexico, Central America and the Caribbean Sea islands. South America contains Argentina, Bolivia, Brazil (which occupies almost half the continent), Chile, Colombia, Ecuador, French Guiana, Guyana, Paraguay, Peru, Suriname, Uruguay and Venezuela.

Hurons carry corpses to a mass grave. The Huron believed that mingling their ancestors' bones helped unite their people.

Sympathy cards are sent to the deceased person's family with a personal message of sadness and support.

Expressing Sympathy

North Americans today follow different death rituals. The casket, lying in a funeral home, may be left open for friends and relatives to visit and pay their respects. Friends and relatives send large garlands of flowers, cards and food to show sympathy and support for the deceased person's family. Sometimes photographs of the dead person are on display, and objects meaningful to or associated with the person are placed in the casket. After a memorial service in a church or the funeral home and the burial or cremation, the mourners often share a meal.

On Memorial Day, a family member visits the grave of a man who was a veteran of the Korean War.

Visiting Cemeteries

Many people visit the burial places of their loved ones regularly to pay homage, pray or find some comfort. On special occasions, such as the birthday of the deceased, anniversary of his or her death or religious holidays, mourners bring flowers and other decorations to place at the grave. On Memorial Day, when Americans honour those who have died in wars, a wreath is placed on the Tomb of the Unknown Soldier in Arlington National Cemetery in Virginia. The individual graves of fallen soldiers are also decorated by loved ones with flags and flowers.

The grave of Elvis Presley at his home in Memphis has become a shrine for millions of his fans.

The gravesite of John F. Kennedy (1917-1963), who served as U.S. president. The body of his wife, Jacqueline Bouvier Kennedy Onassis (1929-1994), was buried next to him.

Memorial Shrines

Many graves and memorial sites in North America have become modern-day shrines. In 1982, following the Vietnam War (1957-1975), the Vietnam Veterans Memorial was dedicated in Washington, D.C. The names of at least 58,000 dead or missing soldiers are inscribed on the black granite wall. Elvis Presley, who was called the "king of rock 'n' roll", died in 1977 at the age of 42. He is buried at Graceland, his mansion home in Memphis, Tennessee. Since his death, millions of devoted fans have visited his grave. Assassinated in Dallas in 1963, John F. Kennedy, the 35th president of the United States, is buried at Arlington National Cemetery in Virginia. Many people continue to pay their respects at the grave, which is adorned with an eternal flame.

IN NEW ORLEANS, WHERE JAZZ MUSIC ORIGINATED, it became traditional for jazz bands to accompany funeral processions. On the way to the cemetery, the band usually played a sad, slow tune as it followed the casket. On the way back, however, the jazz players would strike up a lively number, such as "When the Saints Go Marching In". These jazz funerals became popular attractions.

Día de Los Muertos in Mexico

Sweet skulls are made of sugar for children to enjoy on Day of the Dead.

The Mexican Día de Los Muertos (Day of the Dead) is based on an Aztec festival dedicated to Mictlantecuhtli, ruler of the land of the dead. The festival included feasts, dances, offerings to honour the dead and sacrifices to the god of war, Huitzilopochtli. It is celebrated by Mexican immigrants and people of Mexican descent around the world. In the Aztec calendar, the festival fell in the ninth month (July or August on the Western calendar). After the Spanish conquest of Mexico, the festival was moved to November 2 (All Souls' Day) and mixed with Christian traditions. The modern Day of the Dead, when the dead supposedly return to the world of the living, represents a fascinating blend of cultures.

A woman paints skeleton decorations. Although Mexicans enjoy making fun of death, they never forget to honour their ancestors.

Mictlantecuhtli rules the underworld, known as Mictlan, according to Aztec mythology.

Offerings to the Dead

Beginning in mid-October, Mexican bakeries, market stalls and stores are filled with all sorts of food and toys in shapes or featuring symbols associated with death. Many are in the shape of skeletons, which are usually shown laughing through their bony skulls. There are papier-mâché figurines, wreaths and candles, many decorated with paper or silk flowers. Although many of the goods are given to children as presents, they are intended as offerings to the dead on their special day.

Home Altars

Before the festival, many families put up an altar in memory of their dead relatives. Photographs of the dead are placed on the altar. The family also may decorate the altar with tissue paper cut-outs and sugar skulls with the name of a dead person inscribed using icing and flowers—especially orange and yellow marigolds, the traditional flower of the dead. A selection of favourite food is put out, and incense and candles are lit to help the spirits of the dead find their way home. A candle is lit for each dead relative, and there is always one extra in case anyone has been forgotten. A washbasin and towel may be provided, so that visiting spirits can freshen up before their meal.

A calavera (skull) is always the centre of attention on the table and altar.

Candles are lit to show dead spirits the way.

Graves are specially decorated for the festival.

Honouring the Dead

On November 2, families gather at cemeteries for festive reunions with the living and to honour the dead. Bells are rung to call on the dead spirits. Many people bring baskets of food, and there is always plenty for everyone at the family picnic. In the evening, candles light up the graves so that the spirits can find their living relatives. Some people keep an all-night vigil, but many have a family supper at home. This usually includes the special treat called bread of the dead.

Preparing the Cemetery

Relatives clean and tidy up the graves at the family burial plot in the local cemetery well ahead of the festival. Weeds are pulled out/up, tombstones are washed, and the graves are decorated. Many are adorned with wreaths, garlands and crosses made of marigold petals. Childrens' graves may be decorated with paper streamers. Often, a trail of petals is laid from the cemetery to the house of a dead child. The spirits of these angelitos (little angels) are the first to return on November 1 (All Saints' Day).

BREAD OF THE DEAD

- 60 ml milk
- 60 g butter
- 60 ml warm water
- 450 g flour
- 1¼ teaspoons active dry yeast
- ½ teaspoon salt

- 2 teaspoons aniseed
- 100 g sugar
- 2 eggs, beaten
- 60 ml fresh orange juice
- 1 tablespoon orange peel

Heat milk and butter in a saucepan until the butter melts. Remove from heat and add water. Combine 150 g of flour, yeast, salt, aniseed and half the sugar in a bowl. Stir in milk mixture. Mix in the eggs plus 150 g more flour. Gradually add the last 150 g flour. Knead the dough until smooth and elastic (about 10 minutes). Place in a bowl, cover with a cloth and let rise in a warm place for an hour. Shape the dough into a round loaf, place on a baking tray, cover and let rise for another hour. Bake in a preheated 180°C/350°F/gas 4 oven for 40 minutes. To make glaze, combine remaining sugar, orange juice and peel, then boil over medium heat for 2 minutes. Brush over bread while still warm.

African Spirits of the Dead

A traditional healer and priest wears his religious robes that include fetishes (spiritual charms) around his waist. These help him make contact with the spirits of dead ancestors.

Africa

Africa is a vast continent with many different peoples, cultures and religions. Traditions surrounding death differ as well. Some funeral customs and rites follow those of Christianity and Islam, the two major world religions practised in Africa. Other customs and rites are much older and vary among societies. Most ancient traditions, however, express the belief that the dead are powerful and accessible to the living. Traditional priests and healers help the spirits of the dead pass back and forth between their world and the world of the living.

Spirits

When a person dies, his or her spirit has to enter a new world through a dangerous entrance. The spirit has to be helped through with the correct rituals. Sculptures are cared for to keep spirits happy in many parts of West Africa. The Fon of Benin keep hundreds of metal spirit sculptures called asen. The Ashanti of Ghana have personal stools that serve as small ancestral shrines. When they die, their stools are ritually blackened to show they have joined the ancestors.

Jukun ancestor figures from Nigeria act as a link between the priest and the spirit world. They are displayed at ceremonies, especially funerals, and in times of danger.

A Surma woman wears a traditional lip plate. The Surma consider lip plates a sign of wealth. The plates are buried with them when they die.

Gifts to the Spirit World

Sacrifices of animals and fish are often made to the spirit world to ensure that a dead person's spirit will be accepted into it. In many societies, liquids are offered to show respect for the deceased person and the spirit world. These liquids are called libations. The Surma (also called Suri) of Ethiopia and Sudan pour milk into the deceased's ears. The Banyankole people of Uganda sprinkle bulls' blood around the house of the deceased to purify the house and protect the family. Libations are often taken to shrines that hold images of ancestral spirits that live in nature. Many traditional African societies rely on agriculture for their survival. So offering libations to the spirits helps ensure good crops and healthy animals.

AFRICA

Africa lies south of Europe and west of Asia and contains 53 independent countries. Tropical rain forests dominate western and central Africa. The world's largest desert, the Sahara, stretches across northern Africa. Africa also has the world's longest river—the Nile. Much of the continent is grassland. In the north, most of the people are Arabs. The great majority of the African population lives south of the Sahara.

The Faces of Spirits

In many societies, people wear masks while performing funeral rituals. These events are known as masquerades. Funeral masks represent spirits of the supernatural world. These can include ancestors, gods, legendary figures, forces of the natural world and the beings or spirits that created it. The Dogon of Mali wear masks to prepare the deceased for their next life. West African Yoruba dancers wear colourful costumes to honour and summon the spirits of their ancestors. Elaborate masks are a prominent part of these costumes. The colours, patterns and texture of the fabrics and the intricate carving of the masks are very important because, according to Yoruba belief, the costumed dancers actually become the ancestral spirits during the ritual dances.

A wooden mask with a double cross on top is worn by a Dogon masked dancer from West Africa. The dancer acts out the balance between heaven and Earth.

Dogon masked dancers represent cremation and every aspect of life at a funeral.

A dance mask from Gabon represents a dead person's spirit. Masks such as this appear in dances performed during mourning ceremonies.

Dancing for the Dead

Ceremonial dances give a dead spirit its last glimpse of Earth. They also please the world of ancestor spirits. The Dogon include dancing in funeral ceremonies that may last up to six days. Some dancers perform on stilts. In West Africa, Senufo masked dancers appear from the forest to protect the world of the living from the spirits. The forest represents the place of wisdom. Some of the dancers perform acrobatic movements that represent such creatures as buffalo and crocodiles. Some of the dancers perform in pairs, dancing around the village to chase away any evil spirits. In most African societies, death is considered a bad omen, as well as a release into the afterlife.

African Funeral Music

Music is a central part of funerals in many African societies. In some communities, particularly in West Africa, masked societies also provide the sacred mourning music. Drums are especially important. Certain drum tones recount the life of the deceased. Sometimes they help release the spirit from the body and send it to the world of the dead. Among the Yoruba, talking drums also send messages from the dead to the living. These drums have strings attached to their drum skins. When the strings are squeezed or released, the skin is tightened or relaxed. This movement creates different tones when the skin is beaten or tapped. People can understand the drum's messages because the tones are like those used in Yoruba speech.

Shona musicians from Zimbabwe play their drums for the funeral of a villager. The drums are used to communicate with the spirit world.

Tall, carved plank masks are worn by the Bwa of Burkina Faso in West Africa. They mark the end of the mourning period. Long fibre cloaks hang down from the masks to cover the dancers' bodies.

Traditional African Funerals

Traditional African funerals and mourning periods usually include music, song, dance, masquerades and offerings. All these help the spirit of the dead person move into his or her new world. They also show that people care about the dead person. In addition, these rituals help ensure that the dead spirit will return to help the living in times of trouble. The spirits of all the ancestors are honoured at remembrance ceremonies. Spirit masks are sometimes worn on these occasions as well as at funerals.

A Chance to Say Goodbye

Funerals not only enable family and friends to say goodbye to the deceased, but also help introduce the person's spirit to the afterlife. The person's corpse is bathed, dressed, decorated and perfumed. People visit the deceased and offer gifts and money. Musicians play ritual music, and dances are often performed, especially by traditional priests. The Senufo people of West Africa believe that a person's spirit lingers in the community after death. A funeral ceremony helps the spirit move away from the village and into the world of the dead, where it belongs.

A Senufo statue called a Pombibele is used during the funeral ceremonies of members of the Poro society. Some groups use them as rhythm pounders for dancers. Others stand them in the middle of the ceremonial ground.

At a Senufo funeral, a rod wrapped in a cloth is laid on a special table to represent the deceased. A Yarajo masked dancer uses his spiritual contacts to find out who should be allowed to attend the secret Poro death rituals.

Fantasy Coffins

The Ga people of Ghana often bury their dead in fantastic, dramatic carved coffins. These coffins are special to the dead person. They may show the person's occupation or hobby. They may also show something funny or even fearsome about a person's character! The coffins help people cross over the bridge of life into the world of the dead.

This coffin in the shape of a cow was made for a dairy farmer in Ghana. Coffins may be made into nearly any shape, including planes, boats, cars–anything! Bird coffins are often used for people who held power.

Carpenters in a coffin workshop in Ghana attach a lining to a fantasy coffin in the shape of a chicken. A chicken is often used to represent a mother, who protects her chicks.

Mourning

Africa's hot climate makes a dead body decay rapidly, so mourning has to take place quickly, even though some people may have to travel far to mourn their loved one. The Khoikhoi from Namibia in southern Africa wail beside a dying or dead person for many hours, but the Ashanti from Ghana mourn quietly. They want the spirit to hear their prayers. Family members of the deceased wear precious gold jewellery and dark red, black or orange clothes. Mourning bands are also worn around the head. The bands are believed to prevent evil spirits from ruling their thoughts during the funeral. In Burkina Faso, Senufo hunters mourn the loss of a fellow hunter with a dramatic representation of a hunt. Some of the men dress in animal costumes, while others pretend to hunt them down. The masked performance is believed to free the soul of the deceased.

A huge gold pendant is often worn by Ashanti mourners at Ghanaian funerals. Gold symbolises eternal life.

A Dogon spirit mask of West Africa is made mainly of cowrie shells. Cowrie shells look like eyes and are worn to scare away evil spirits.

The meeting house (marae) is the focal point of Maori community life. Intricately carved in wood, it is used for weddings, funerals and reunions.

Australasia and Oceania

Funeral Rituals in Oceania

The aboriginal people of Australia and Oceania treat their ancestors and dead relatives with great respect. Their journey from Earth to the next life is commemorated in many ways and often results in impressive art forms that honour the deceased and their spiritual ancestors. In the Maori culture, the deceased is surrounded by family and friends before being buried. Elaborate face and body painting forms an important part of the mourning process for many native people of the Oceanic islands.

This Maori lizard amulet, made from a human skull and shell, was made for protection against the evil powers of Whiro, the god of darkness, evil and death. According to Maori legend, Whiro controls the evil spirits that cause illness among the living, while the goddess Hine-nui-te-po protects the dead and rules the underworld.

Maori Tangihanga Ritual

A Maori tangihanga (funeral) is one of the best preserved and most important of traditional Maori rituals. They are always held at the community's meeting house, called a marae. Maoris believe that the body of the deceased, the tupapaku, should not be left alone at any time after death. Friends and family, often coming from far away, meet in the marae and stay with the body until burial takes place in the nearby urupa (cemetery). On arrival at the marae, the coffin is greeted by the wailing of old women, and over the next few days, visitors arrive to pay their respects to the deceased, whose coffin is left open. Speeches are made in the Maori language to help send the deceased to the land of ancestors. During this time, relatives and visitors also talk, joke, sing and settle arguments.

During a Maori tangihanga, friends and family of the deceased gather together for two or three days, talking and singing songs. Close relatives sleep at the marae, which is decorated with carvings and photographs of their ancestors.

AUSTRALASIA AND OCEANIA

Australasia and Oceania lie east of Asia and west of the Americas. Australasia refers to Australia, New Guinea, New Zealand and other nearby islands. New Guinea and New Zealand are also considered as part of the Pacific Islands, or Oceania. Oceania is a name given to a group of many thousands of islands scattered across the Pacific Ocean. New Guinea is the largest island in the group. It contains Irian Jaya, which is a part of Indonesia, and the independent country of Papua New Guinea. Islands near the mainland of Asia (Indonesia, Japan, the Philippines) are part of Asia. Islands near North and South America (the Aleutians, the Galapagos) are grouped with those continents. Australia is itself a continent.

Irian Jayan Death Rituals

The traditional head-hunting tribes of the Asmat believed that death is always caused by an evil enemy. Their most expressive examples of art are bis poles, which are dedicated to their ancestors.

Aboriginal Funeral Customs

Aboriginal culture is steeped in the belief of spirit ancestors. When an Aborigine dies, the sign of his or her clan is painted on the abdomen. This practice connects the deceased to his or her ancestral source. Mourning rituals and burial differed among each tribe. Disposing of the body might include simple burial, cremation or leaving it in a cave or on a high platform. Among the Aboriginal Tiwi tribe, funeral rituals called Pukimani can last weeks or even months after death. The Tiwi follow formalised codes of behaviour out of respect for the spirit of the deceased. The main event of the ceremony, the carving of elaborate funeral poles, takes place months after death. Once completed, these poles are erected around the grave, and serve as the focus of ritual dancing and funeral chants.

A bis pole was carved from mangrove wood in honour of an important Asmat person who has died. When the people have had enough time to avenge the evil that caused the death, they take the poles into the forest and let them decay.

A Papua New Guinean widow wears a necklace of cowrie shells and paints blue-gray mud on her face as a sign of mourning for her husband.

Funeral poles mark a burial site of the Tiwi people on Melville Island off northern Australia. The funeral poles are painted bright colours and some are as high as 4 metres (13 feet).

Malagan Ceremonies in New Ireland

The island of New Ireland in Papua New Guinea holds complex ceremonial death rituals called malagan. This is a second burial ceremony that both commemorates the dead and introduces new initiates to society. A series of funeral rites are performed during this ceremony, which tries to free the soul from the dead body so that it may go to its final resting place. Masks called tatanua masks are made for the occasion and are given the name of a dead person. Carved in wood, they are made in honour of a deceased person and given as a final funeral offering.

This wooden tatanua mask is decorated with a colourful headdress of cane, and its eyes are made from snail shells, giving it a terrifying expression.

Glossary

Afterlife Life after death.

Ancestor A family member from a preceding generation to whom you are directly related, for example, a grandfather or great-grandfather.

Anoint To rub or apply a lotion, often oil, to the skin during a ceremony.

Ashes What remains of a human body when burned.

Bereaved The state of having lost a close family member to death.

Bier A stand on which a dead body or coffin is placed before burial or cremation.

Blessing Divine favour or protection. An approval or wish for happiness.

Burial The act or ceremony of placing a dead body in a grave or tomb.

Catacombs An underground network of passages and chambers that serves as a burial place.

Cemetery A piece of land set aside for the burial of dead bodies.

Ceremony The celebration of an important event with an act or series of acts that follows a set of instructions established by a religion, culture or country.

Coffin The container in which a dead body is placed to be buried.

Commemorate To honour the memory of a special historical or religious event with a celebration or ceremony.

Communism A political, social and economic system in which most or all property is owned by the state and is supposed to be shared by all.

Condolence The expression of sympathy after a death.

Confession The admission of sins or wrongdoings.

Corpse The dead body of a human being.

Cortege A solemn procession.

Cremation The act of burning a dead body to ashes.

Deceased Dead. A dead person.

Descendant A blood relative of a previous generation. A child is a descendant of his or her parents, grandparents, great-grandparents and so on.

Embalm The act of preserving a dead body.

Enlightenment The act of receiving spiritual or intellectual insight or information.

Exile The state of having been forced to leave one's native country.

Funeral A religious or other ceremony that usually takes place before a dead body is buried or cremated (burned to ashes).

Grave A hole dug in the ground where a dead body is buried.

Grief Emotional distress and suffering, especially felt after the death of someone close.

Hearse A vehicle used to transport a coffin.

Icon An image of a god or goddess that is considered sacred and is given special respect.

Immortal Living forever, never dying.

Incense A material that produces perfumed smoke when burned, usually made from plant products.

Legend A story from a time in the past.

Lunar calendar A calendar that marks the passing of years by following the phases of the moon. Lunar calendars are still used today by the members of some religions and cultures.

Masquerade A gathering of people wearing masks and costumes to celebrate a special event or occasion.

Meditation A time of quiet thought and spiritual reflection.

Memorial An object, such as a statue or place, which is a reminder of a dead person or past event.

Minority A group of people with their own identity who are outnumbered by larger groups.

Monastery A place where a community of religious people, such as monks, live.

Monk A man who has separated himself from ordinary ways of life to devote himself to his religion.

Mortuary A place where a dead body is kept before a funeral. Denoting death or burial.

Mourning A period following a person's death, during which people express deep sorrow and may perform special rituals in observance of that death.

Mummy A dead body preserved to prevent it from decaying.

Pall-bearer A person who walks with or helps to carry a coffin.

Pilgrimage A journey taken to visit a holy place.

Plague A fatal disease that spreads easily and kills many people.

Procession A parade held for a religious ceremony or ritual.

Purification The act of cleansing a person or object,

often through ceremony or ritual.

Pyre A pile of wood for burning a dead body during a funeral ceremony.

Recite To say something, such as a prayer or verse, to an audience or in a group of people.

Reincarnation The rebirth of a soul into a new body.

Reliquary A small box or container for precious relics and objects.

Ritual A set of repeated actions done in a precise way, usually with a solemn meaning or significance.

Sacrament A ceremony or practice that is an outward sign that a faithful worshipper is receiving God's blessing.

Sacred Holy or precious.

Sacrifice The killing of an animal which is offered to a god or gods as part of worship.

Scripture Sacred, religious writing or a passage from the Bible.

Shrine A small chapel, altar, or sacred place of worship.

Shroud The cloth or garment in which a dead person is wrapped for burial.

Sin An immoral, wrongful act.

Soul The spiritual part of a human being.

Spirit A good or bad supernatural being or force.

Sympathy The sharing of someone's sorrows and sad feelings.

Tomb A structure, often above the ground, where a dead body is housed.

Tombstone A stone or other marker that marks a tomb or grave.

Unction The act of anointing a person with oil in a religious practice.

Underworld A world that lies below the world of the living, also called hell.

Urn A vase used to hold the ashes of a cremated dead person.

Wail A long, loud cry because of pain or grief.

Widow A woman whose husband is dead and who has not married again. A widower is a man whose wife is dead and who has not married again.

Wreath A circle of flowers or leaves.

Index